GOOD FOOD

Fruit

Julia Adams

Explore the world with **Popcorn** — your complete first non-fiction library.

Look out for more titles in the Popcorn range. All books have the same format of simple text and striking images. Text is carefully matched to the pictures to help readers to identify and understand key vocabulary.
www.waylandbooks.co.uk/popcorn

First published in 2010 by Wayland
This paperback edition published in 2012 by Wayland
Reprinted by Wayland in 2012

Wayland
Hachette Children's Books
338 Euston Road
London NW1 3BH

Wayland Australia
Level 17/207 Kent Street
Sydney NSW 2000

Editor and Picture Researcher: Julia Adams
Designer: Paul Cherrill
Food and Nutrition Consultant: Ester Davies
Photo Models: Asha Francis; Lydia Washbourne

British Library Cataloguing in Publication Data
Adams, Julia.
   Fruit. -- (Popcorn. Good food)
   1. Fruit--Juvenile literature. 2. Fruit in human nutrition--Juvenile literature.
   I. Title II. Series
   641.3'4-dc22

ISBN 978 0 7502 6758 8

Wayland is a division of Hachette Children's Books, an Hachette UK company, www. hachette.co.uk

Photographs:

Alamy: Spyros Bourboulis 1/9, Ed Young 10, Mick Rock 11, Helen Sessions 15; Andy Crawford: 2, 13, 16, 20, 22, 23; iStock: monkeybusinessimages 4, ktaylorg 19/OFC; Shutterstock: Kruchankova Maya 5, Dino O. 6, shalunishka 7, karnizz 8, Marta P. 12, Hannamariah 14, Monkey Business Images 17, Feng Yu 18, Gelpi 21;

Contents

Good for you

Everyone needs to eat the right kind of food to stay healthy. The food we cook and eat comes from plants and animals.

Fresh food such as vegetables, fruit and grains can be eaten in many ways.

Fruit is good for us because it has vitamins and minerals. Our bodies need these to keep the heart healthy, and to help us stop catching colds.

Eating lots of fresh fruit and vegetables is good for you.

There are many different kinds of fruit. How many do you know?

What is fruit?

Apples, blackberries and oranges are all fruit. They come from plants. Fruit can be many shapes, sizes and colours.

Can you name all the fruits in this picture?

We eat the flesh of a fruit. The flesh can be soft or hard. It is often sweet and juicy. We can eat the skin of some fruits, too.

You need to peel the skin off a banana before you eat it!

How fruit grows

Fruit grows on many different kinds
of plants. It grows on trees and bushes.
In spring, these plants grow flowers.
The flowers are called blossom.

This apple tree is covered in blossom.

8

After the blossom falls off, the fruit begins to grow. When the fruit is ripe, it is ready to pick and eat.

Apples can be red, green, yellow or brown.

 Farming fruit

Most of the fruit that we eat is grown on farms. Farmers grow the fruit plants in rows. This makes it easier to pick the fruit when it is ripe.

These are rows of grapevines.

The ripe fruit is picked by hand or by a machine. Then the fruit is packed into boxes and taken to shops.

These grapes have just been picked.

Citrus fruits

Oranges, grapefruit and lemons are all citrus fruits. They grow on trees in hot countries.

Lemons are green at first. They are ripe when they turn yellow.

Citrus fruits have a thick, shiny skin.
You have to peel them to eat them.
Citrus fruits are very juicy.

You can squeeze
citrus fruits,
like oranges,
to make
fruit juice.

Try
different citrus
fruits like grapefruit,
limes, tangerines
and lemons.
What do they
taste like?

Orchard fruits

Apples, pears, nectarines and plums are all orchard fruits. They grow on trees. Farmers grow these fruit trees on a piece of land called an orchard.

The fruit trees in an orchard are planted in rows. These are nectarine trees.

Many orchard fruits can be pressed to make fruit juices. They can also be dried to make a tasty snack.

Can you guess which dried orchard fruits these are?

Tropical fruits

Some fruits only grow in hot places. Tropical fruits are from countries that are warm and wet all year round.

How many of these tropical fruits do you know?

We often add tropical fruits to desserts. We also use them in smoothies and in milkshakes.

Tropical fruits are tasty in a fruit salad.

Did you know that bananas can be yellow, red or purple?

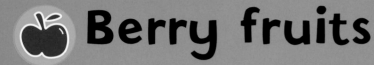 # Berry fruits

Gooseberries, strawberries and blackcurrants are all berries. They grow on bushes and trees.

These blueberries grow on trees.

We eat berries in cereals and desserts. Some berries, like strawberries, can also be used to make jam.

Can you name any berries that are made into jam?

Vegetable fruits

Tomatoes, cucumbers, pumpkins and peppers are called vegetable fruits. This is because they are not very sweet.

Vegetable fruits grow from a flower and have seeds, just like other fruit.

We use vegetable fruits in many savoury dishes. We can eat them raw, or roast, bake or fry them.

Tomatoes, cucumbers, peppers and avocados are great in salads.

Make a fruit salad

You will need:
- kitchen roll • knife
- chopping board • bowl
- one banana • one kiwi
- one or two apples
- one orange

Follow this recipe to make a delicious fruit salad as a snack or for breakfast.

1. Wash the apples and dry them with some kitchen towel.

2. Peel the banana.

3. Use the knife to chop the banana into slices. Ask an adult to help you with this. Add the slices to the bowl.

4. Ask an adult to peel the kiwi for you. Cut it in half and slice it. Add the slices to the bowl.

5. After an adult has helped you cut the apples into quarters, slice each quarter. Add the pieces to the bowl.

6. Ask an adult to cut an orange in half. Squeeze the orange over the fruit in the bowl. Mix the orange juice with the fruit. Enjoy!

Glossary

blossom the flower of a plant

flesh the soft inside of a fruit that we eat

grapevine the plant that grapes grow on

minerals substances in food that keep our bodies healthy

ripe when a fruit or vegetable is ready to eat

seeds parts of plants that grow to form new plants

vitamins substances in food that help keep our bodies healthy and stop us from catching colds

Index